SUPER CUTE!

Baby Sheep

by Christina Leaf

BELLWETHER MEDIA • MINNEAPOLIS, MN

Note to Librarians, Teachers, and Parents:

Blastoff! Readers are carefully developed by literacy experts and combine standards-based content with developmentally appropriate text.

Level 1 provides the most support through repetition of high-frequency words, light text, predictable sentence patterns, and strong visual support.

Level 2 offers early readers a bit more challenge through varied simple sentences, increased text load, and less repetition of high-frequency words.

Level 3 advances early-fluent readers toward fluency through increased text and concept load, less reliance on visuals, longer sentences, and more literary language.

Level 4 builds reading stamina by providing more text per page, increased use of punctuation, greater variation in sentence patterns, and increasingly challenging vocabulary.

Level 5 encourages children to move from "learning to read" to "reading to learn" by providing even more text, varied writing styles, and less familiar topics.

Whichever book is right for your reader, Blastoff! Readers are the perfect books to build confidence and encourage a love of reading that will last a lifetime!

This edition first published in 2014 by Bellwether Media, Inc.

No part of this publication may be reproduced in whole or in part without written permission of the publisher. For information regarding permission, write to Bellwether Media, Inc., Attention: Permissions Department, 5357 Penn Avenue South, Minneapolis, MN 55419.

Library of Congress Cataloging-in-Publication Data

Leaf, Christina, author.
  Baby Sheep / by Christina Leaf.
    pages cm. – (Blastoff! Readers. Super Cute!)
  Summary: "Developed by literacy experts for students in kindergarten through grade three, this book introduces baby sheep to young readers through leveled text and related photos"– Provided by publisher.
  Audience: Ages 5-8.
  Audience: K to grade 3.
  Includes bibliographical references and index.
  ISBN 978-1-60014-978-8 (hardcover : alk. paper)
  1. Lambs–Juvenile literature. 2. Animals–Infancy–Juvenile literature. I. Title.
  SF376.5.L43 2014
  636.3'07–dc23
                              2013050257

Printed in the United States of America, North Mankato, MN:

Table of Contents

Lambs!

A baby sheep is called a lamb. It has curly hair called **wool**.

Many lambs are born on farms. A **ewe** has one or two babies at a time.

The lamb stands soon after birth. Mom helps it up.

The lamb is shaky at first. Soon it runs with the **flock**.

It likes to jump and play with other lambs.

Young bighorn
sheep love
to climb!

Time to Eat

A lamb **bleats** to tell mom it is hungry. She feeds it her milk.

Older lambs **graze** to eat. Then they chew their **cud**.

A lamb lies down in a **pasture** to rest. It curls its legs in. Goodnight, little lamb!

Glossary

bleats—makes a noise that sounds like a shaky cry

cud—food that is chewed again after being in the belly

ewe—a female sheep

flock—a group of sheep

graze—to feed on grasses and other plants

pasture—a field with grasses to graze on

wool—the soft, thick hair of sheep

To Learn More

AT THE LIBRARY

Kawa, Katie. *Lambs*. New York, N.Y.: Gareth Stevens Pub., 2012.

Kopp, Megan. *Sheep*. New York, N.Y.: Weigl, 2013.

Stiefel, Chana. *Sheep on the Family Farm*. Berkeley Heights, N.J.: Enslow, 2014.

ON THE WEB

Learning more about sheep is as easy as 1, 2, 3.

1. Go to www.factsurfer.com.

2. Enter "sheep" into the search box.

3. Click the "Surf" button and you will see a list of related web sites.

With factsurfer.com, finding more information is just a click away.

Index

The images in this book are reproduced through the courtesy of: April Turner, front cover; Chris Westwood, pp. 4-5; Erica Olsen/ FLPA, pp. 6-7, 12-13; Edwin Remsberg/ Agefotostock, pp. 8-9; Exactostock/ SuperStock, pp. 10-11; milehightraveler, pp. 14-15; Hanneke Luijting/ Getty Images, pp. 16-17; F1 Online/ SuperStock, pp. 18-19; H. Tuller, pp. 20-21.